HUDSON RIVER

AN ADVENTURE FROM THE MOUNTAINS TO THE SEA

BY PETER LOURIE

ILLUSTRATED WITH FULL-COLOR PHOTOGRAPHS

TO: HUDSON
THE PICTURES IN HERE
ARE GLORIEOUS +
MAYBE ONE DAY YOU
CAN VENTURE HERE!
LOVE,
TESS
DIMOTO

Contents

HUDSON RIVER

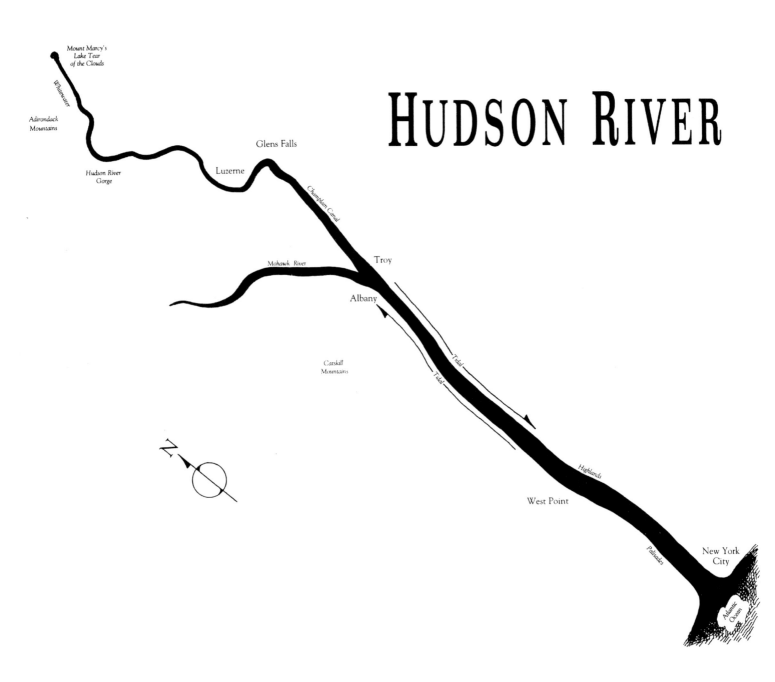

Mount Marcy's
Lake Tear
of the Clouds

Whitewater

Adirondack
Mountains

Hudson River
Gorge

Luzerne

Glens Falls

Champlain Canal

Mohawk River

Troy

Albany

Catskill
Mountains

Tidal

Tidal

Highlands

West Point

Palisades

New York
City

Atlantic
Ocean

N

Prologue

Henry Hudson called it the great River of the Mountains. Born as a mountain brook, it picks up speed and volume and runs fiercely through a wilderness of pines and dangerous rapids. Then the river evens out. Below Albany the Hudson becomes a huge tidal arm of the sea. While the first half of the river plummets more than 4,000 feet, the second half is nearly flat, dropping only a few feet to the Atlantic Ocean!

In its 315-mile journey to the sea, the Hudson is many rivers, from wilderness stream and old log-driving route to barge canal and commercial shipping lane. Long ago it was even a hiding place for pirates and treasure.

Mapping the trail to Lake Tear of the Clouds.

The Hudson seemed to me like an uncharted river waiting to be explored. No one had ever canoed the entire river. So I planned a canoe trip from the river's source, a pond high in the mist and ragged spruce trees of the Adirondack Mountains, to the river's mouth at Battery Park on the southern tip of Manhattan. To reach the source of the Hudson I would have to carry my canoe up a long trail to Lake Tear of the Clouds, near the summit of Mount Marcy, the highest mountain in New York State. For the first leg of my journey I hired an Adirondack guide named Ernie LaPrairie. He would help me up to Lake Tear and then guide me through the seventy-five miles of the Hudson's treacherous headwaters. After that, I would canoe 240 miles alone to the sea!

CHAPTER ONE

The Mountains

JUNE 11 – PORTAGE

AT DAWN ERNIE AND I SET OUT ON A WIDE TRAIL in the heart of the high peaks near the town of Newcomb. Because it is impossible to canoe the beginning of the river, we had planned a two-day hike to Lake Tear just to see the river's source.

The morning was gray, cool, and misty. I hoisted onto my back a sixty-pound pack stuffed with all our camping gear. Ernie turned the eighteen-foot canoe over onto his shoulders, and we started off following Calamity Brook. Then we hiked along the edge of the green-tinted Opalescent River to the cascade of Feldspar Brook, which tumbles out of Lake Tear of the Clouds. The trail was steep. The higher we climbed, the fewer hemlock and balsam trees we saw, and the more tattered and wind-torn the spruce became. Walking the last few hundred yards was like walking on top of the world.

An aerial view of Lake Tear of the Clouds.

Lake Tear of the Clouds as seen by Colvin in 1872.

Lake Tear emerged through the trees near the summit of Mount Marcy. Sitting on Marcy's shoulder, at nearly 4,300 feet, Lake Tear of the Clouds seemed to me as forlorn and beautiful a place as it must have been when early surveyor Verplanck Colvin first described it in 1872 as "a minute, unpretending tear of the clouds… a lonely pool, shivering in the breezes of the mountains."

The Algonquian Indians called Mount Marcy Tahawus, or "Cloud Splitter," because it was so high it pierced the clouds.

Feldspar Outlet: The beginning of the Hudson River.

It was too late in the day and too cold and rainy to paddle on the lake, so we hid our paddles in the woods and pulled our canoe under some spruce. We filled our canteens from the Feldspar outlet that is the very beginning of the Hudson River. Then, racing against the oncoming darkness, we hiked back to a lean-to we had passed on the trail going up. The sign on the wall of the lean-to read "Beware: A Big Bear Got Our Food Here," but the night passed with no sign of bears.

JUNE 12-LAKE TEAR OF THE CLOUDS

Adirondack weather can change quickly: the morning was sun bright and gold in a flawless blue sky. We hiked back to the lake to find Marcy's bright peak blazing above us. In our sleek canoe we shot across the pond with only a few paddle strokes. Trudging down from Lake Tear, I kept thinking about the rapids that lay ahead. They really scared me—I had canoed in whitewater only once before!

Down the trail to the river.

JUNE 13 - LINING THE CANOE

We launched the canoe in the Hudson where it first becomes navigable. For nine miles we canoed on a tranquil stream: this far north, the Hudson is only fifty feet wide. The calm black-green water reflected the sky, the pines, and the distant mountains so precisely I could hardly distinguish up from down.

Canoeing Lake Tear.

*It's hard to believe this is the same river that
passes like a wide brown ocean beneath the
George Washington Bridge.*

The river runs through rocky passages.

Getting ready for whitewater.

"Lining" the canoe.

We heard a distant roar ahead of us—it was the sound of the rapids where the Hudson takes its first dive through treacherous rocks. We pulled our canoe to shore and prepared for whitewater battle. The water was freezing cold from the spring runoff, so we dressed in wetsuits and life vests. We put on our crash helmets and pushed out into the foam. The wind rose off the swirling water as the river thundered through rocky passages. But it was impossible to run the river for very long because of the rocks, so we had to get out and take turns "lining" the canoe. While holding one line tied to the stern and one to the bow, we would shoot the canoe into the rapids and give the lines a tug when the canoe began to stray toward danger.

From rock to rock we surfed, plowed, slalomed, schussed, and drove our canoe downriver.

JUNE 14 – WHITEWATER

For safety in the whitewater ahead, the following day we lashed two extra paddles to the inside of the canoe. We inflated a big yellow air bag and tied it between us to make sure the canoe would ride high in the water if we turned over. Ernie had the important job of "reading" the water, which meant that he had to guide us clear of the rocks before we hit them. He drew his paddle on the right, and I pried on the left. He crossed his paddle to the other side to take the bow around a big rock, and I helped bring the stern around, too. Then quickly we reversed direction, always keeping the canoe parallel to the course of the river. Sometimes, when the river got too wild, we had to back paddle and rethink our approach. Then Ernie would yell, "OK—Paddle!" and we'd dig forward into the spume like men fighting for air.

We came to Blackwell Stillwater, a dark, slow-moving section between rapids. On shore we saw a curious sight: a cross slashed into an old pine tree. Ernie told me that it marked the place where a lumberman had been killed years ago when the Hudson was used to run logs to the sawmills downriver. It seemed a quiet but powerful testament to the bygone days of Adirondack logging.

A cross marks the spot where a lumberman was killed many years ago.

Sitting by the campfire, we could hear the river roaring in the dark.

We camped for the night in the heart of the Gorge at Blue Ledge. Three-hundred-foot bluish cliffs rose high above us. Sitting in the river's deep Blue Ledge Pool were mammoth chunks of broken stone. We ate our dinner in this dramatic setting and then sat by the campfire listening to the loud river roaring in the dark.

Blue Ledge Pool.

More whitewater.

The Mouse.

JUNE 15 – ALMOST MADE IT

It was another gray morning and another whitewater day. We almost made it through the mile-long rapid. For fifteen minutes we maneuvered back and forth and around the rocks. But with a sudden tug the canoe caught a rock, and we swung perpendicular to the flow of the river. As if we didn't have enough trouble, I made the mistake of leaning upstream and the canoe filled with water. We capsized. It was like jumping into a bath of ice cubes. Clumsily I kicked for shore while Ernie swam the canoe to a rock. We emptied the water from the canoe and jumped aboard again. We endured more rapid-fire maneuvering in the constant rush of whitewater before another rock caught the hull and turned us over again. This time we both took a long swim.

Below the Gorge the river's fever died down. We came to gentler whitewater. Here Ernie showed me what the old logging men called the Mouse, a six-foot-long dark patch in a boulder on the bank that looks very much like a real mouse. It is said that one Hudson log-drive boss would look across the river to see whether the rising water had yet touched the tail of the Mouse. If it had, he knew the Hudson was rising fast and it was time to open the dams on the tributaries and make the long push to get the logs down to the Big Boom at Glens Falls. The Big Boom was a chain of logs six hundred feet long and four feet wide that could hold back as many as two million logs.

Rocky cliffs become sloping hills and cow pastures.

JUNE 16 – GOODBYE

Ernie and I left the raging river behind and canoed to the border of the Adirondack Park, where we had to drag the canoe over wide, sandy shoals.

We pulled into shore just above Luzerne's Rockwell Falls, the narrowest part of the Hudson, where it is about twenty feet across. Ernie helped me get the canoe around the falls. Then we stopped for coffee in the village of Luzerne. Ernie and I shook hands and parted company. On the long, hot days of endless solo paddling to come, I would think often of my friend LaPrairie. I would yearn for the wind and the roar of fierce whitewater—because now I had to face a completely different kind of Hudson.

CHAPTER TWO

The Power of the Hudson

JUNE 18 - DAMS

THE RIVER CHANGES DRAMATICALLY AFTER leaving the Adirondack Park just below Luzerne. Its shores are lined with houses and boat docks. Above Luzerne I had the feeling I was canoeing on an ancient, untouched river. But humans and human activity dominate the river below, and aside from a few waterfalls, the river drops much more gradually all the way to the sea.

Without a second paddler, my canoe inched its way forward. I fought a strong wind from the south. It would be a long haul to New York City. I sat on a seat near the middle of the canoe, and I paddled as never before. Without Ernie, it was more difficult to control the light canoe in the brisk wind. I had to paddle three strokes on one side, then quickly paddle three on the other, and so on, back and forth. And there was no time to relax anymore. If I stopped for a moment, the canoe would be blown back upriver.

Troy Lock, the last lock on the Hudson River.

21

A power dam blocked my way.

Suddenly I came upon a huge concrete barrier—a power dam! It was the first of nine, all within thirty miles of one another. I pulled my canoe out on shore and walked through the mill town of Corinth to get around the International Paper Company dam. When I put my canoe back into the water in the deep, quiet pool below, there were no boats anywhere. The river seemed uninhabited. It gave me an eerie feeling. I seemed to be the only moving thing on the surface of the still water. The water looked dead, as if it had no fish in it.

The Spier Falls Dam appeared around a bend in the river. To get around this dam I would have to drag the canoe up a steep hill through a forest. On my first try I started to slide back down, and the canoe knocked me and all my gear into the water. I got up the hill on the second try. After a mile hike I found the river again. Right away I came upon another dam. This time I ran my canoe beside the dam and put in just below the monstrous cement structure. Inside the dam, huge turbines generate electricity. Unlike fossil fuels, hydro-power is a clean energy source: it does not pollute the air, but some believe it can change the ecology of the river.

Big Boom between 1880 and 1890. Millions of logs piled up here before they were sent downriver.

After a long day, I reached a wide part of the river at Glens Falls that was used to hold all the logs driven downriver by Adirondack log-drivers. In the nineteenth and early twentieth centuries the logs piled up at what was called the Big Boom until they were separated and sent to sawmills. The logs would collect in heaps like giant pick-up-sticks, and a brave log driver would have to break a log jam with a pike pole, which looked like a harpoon. The driver would approach the jam cautiously, test a few logs with the pole, then dislodge just the right log to break the jam. A breaking jam broke with a crash, and the log-drivers had to flee for their lives.

At times there were so many logs above the boom that they formed a solid wall three miles long. In the spring of 1859, a flooding Hudson forced the logs at Glens Falls to snap the boom, and half a million logs rushed downstream. The towns below were devastated by water and logs that scattered for forty miles, all the way to Troy.

Tugs and barges can still be seen on the Champlain Canal.

JUNE 19 – LOCKS AND LOCK TENDERS

I reached Lock 7 on the Champlain Canal at Fort Edward. The Champlain Canal was built from Troy to Lake Champlain in the early nineteenth century. Its series of locks allowed barges, tugs, and boats to bypass the rapids in the river. Forty miles of the Hudson River still form part of this canal system. To reach Troy, I would have to pass through seven locks.

The lock tenders were very kind to let my canoe use the locks. Millions of gallons of Hudson water were displaced as my little canoe was "locked" down. The biggest drop was almost twenty feet. The lock chambers are forty-four feet wide and three hundred feet long, big enough for large ships to fit inside.

I watched the huge iron gates of the lock open; then I paddled my canoe into the great chamber. The gates slowly closed behind me, and I felt trapped. The water bulged beneath my hull before it began to drain slowly from the chamber. I hung onto the metal steps along the concrete chamber wall as I sank, ever so gradually, deep, deep into the river. The iron doors in front opened slowly. Water sprayed through the cracks in the big iron doors behind me. The whole Hudson River was being held back by those metal plates, and I paddled quickly downriver to the next lock.

The Hudson River is held back by these huge iron gates.

My canoe getting locked down.

Part of the canal section runs through farm country.

JUNE 20 – A DIFFERENT HUDSON

After Lock 5, I paddled a long, hard thirty miles, sometimes against the wind, all the way to Troy. I paddled this "canal section" of the Hudson through farm country, where the river grows wide and its bends are long and gentle. First I saw farms; then cities appeared along the shore. I passed Waterford, where the Champlain Canal meets the Erie Canal. Here the Mohawk River was pouring its now-polluted water into the River of the Mountains. Dead fish floated in the waves. Dead fish by the hundreds were cast upon the beach. I could not imagine this river's ever having been a wilderness stream.

After the last lock on the Hudson River, I stored my canoe at a marina in Troy for the night and slept in a real bed in a hotel by the water. Again I had come to a different Hudson, a river of industry, big ships, and pollution. But I had also come to a river of tides. For the next 154 miles I would have to wait for the right tide to move ahead. A canoe heading south cannot fight the Hudson when it flows north with its current of five miles an hour or more.

Mechanicville.

Albany.

CHAPTER THREE

Arm of the Sea

JUNE 21 – JOURNEY OF THE HALF MOON

IN THE LATE SUMMER OF 1609, HENRY HUDSON HAD to wait for the tide before he could pull up the anchor of his ship the Half Moon and travel from New York harbor up the great River of the Mountains. He was the first European to sail up the river. Though his ship reached as far north as modern-day Albany in his search for a route to China, Hudson found he could not take it much further because the river became unnavigable.

Hudson would be amazed to see this land today. Along the riverbanks in Troy and Albany I found tankers and docks and sewage treatment plants. Even so, I saw beautiful stretches of thick shrubs and trees still lining the banks between the docks and factories. But environmentalists worry that the untouched sections might not stay that way, and they are always struggling to bring attention to the river, to help people appreciate what has often been so neglected.

Albany, the capital of New York, as seen from the air.

A lighthouse marks the way to port.

JUNE 23 – WATER THAT FLOWS TWO WAYS

Canoeing on a river with tides was like canoeing on a very narrow ocean set between high banks. The smell of the air was brackish, and sea gulls whirled overhead. Along the way I saw lighthouses made of brick marking some of the bigger ports. Great castles and estates with wide manicured lawns sloping down to the water looked like relics from the Middle Ages.

I carried a tide chart to determine when the tide would turn. The tide is influenced by the waning and waxing of the moon, and every day it changes at different times. I canoed only on the ebb tide when all the water in the lower Hudson runs downstream and out into the ocean. The ebb lasts for about six hours, and then the water runs back upriver for another six hours, which is called the flood tide. After the flood, the whole lower Hudson turns back again. It is easy to understand why the Algonquian Indians called the Hudson "Water That Flows Two Ways."

I met freighters and tugs.

JUNE 24 – CLOSE CALLS

Many of the barges, tugs, and freighters run all day and night. They don't have to pay much attention to the tides because their motors are so powerful that they can push their way through anything. When such vessels run with the tide, they can travel as fast as fifteen miles per hour. Twice I paddled for my life to escape the big freighters. And canoeing in the big water of the lower river is dangerous because of the wakes of the ships. A tug pushing a barge can make some huge waves. Many times when a giant ship passed me, I was forced to stop, turn my canoe toward the waves, and ride them slowly with my paddle blade flat out on the water to form a kind of water brace. This helped steady my light canoe in the big swells. But there were times when I was sure I would capsize.

JUNE 25 – THE HUDSON HIGHLANDS

The Hudson passes by three mountain chains: first the Adirondacks, then the Catskills, and then, below the city of Newburgh, the Hudson Highlands, where the river's channel is deepest. The cliffs of Storm King and Breakneck mountains plunge into the water like the cliffs that line the fjords of Norway. So beautiful are the Hudson Highlands that artists often come here to paint. In fact, in the nineteenth century, this part of the river inspired the first American school of painting.

The cliffs of Storm King and Breakneck mountains plunge into the water.

The remains of the rampart that
encircled the island.

The Highlands are home to castles, too. An eccentric arms merchant named Bannerman built his castle on a small island at the turn of the century. Here he stored his collection of guns and other weapons and ammunition. Many years ago the castle was abandoned, and now the state owns the property. I canoed right through the old pillars of the rampart that encircled the island years ago.

Bannerman's Castle.

JUNE 27 – SOME HISTORIC SITES

Fed by tributaries since its beginning at Lake Tear, the Hudson is massive now. Below Newburgh the river grows salty as water from the sea is pushed upstream with the flood tide. This is a historic section of river, too. In 1782 George Washington stationed his headquarters on the riverbank at Newburgh. And just down from Bannerman's Castle is the Military Academy at West Point, founded in 1802. The Hudson bends 90 degrees around the Academy. With a depth of 200 feet or so, this is the deepest part of the river. The area goes by the name of World's End because sailing ships years ago were beset by the rough winds and the swift current. But I needed to apply only a few light strokes of my paddle to get my canoe racing along shore in the ebb tide.

There are legends in these parts. In the late 1600s pirates sailed up the Hudson River looking for safe haven after attacking ships in New York harbor. Some say the buccaneers hid their treasure along the shore. One legend claims that Captain Kidd sailed up the Hudson to bury a treasure not far from the present town of Peekskill.

Indian Point Nuclear Reactor.

John Cronin and his boat the Riverkeeper met me near Indian Point.

JUNE 28 – NUCLEAR POWER

After leaving the Highlands, I canoed past the Indian Point Nuclear Reactor, which seemed a strange sight along the river. John Cronin and his boat, the Riverkeeper, followed me. John is an environmentalist trying to clean up the Hudson. He monitors those who use the river and sues polluters. He has been watching Indian Point very closely because the reactor uses millions of gallons of river water for cooling. Hot water is then discharged back into the river, with great potential to kill large numbers of fish and eventually alter the ecosystem. I canoed over the huge discharge from the reactor, which tore at the boat just as the rapids of the Upper Hudson had. The water swirled and boiled beneath me, tossing my canoe around like a leaf on a pond. John Cronin told me that the river from here to Manhattan had been terribly neglected but has been getting cleaner over the past twenty years, thanks to the work of concerned citizens and environmentalists.

JUNE 29 – FISHING

Near the Tappan Zee Bridge, the river forms a kind of bay that is two miles wide. Looking across the bay is like gazing over a sea. Because it was calm, I canoed to the middle of the channel, but the wind suddenly picked up. The tide was getting strong, and the whitecaps seemed to sweep out of nowhere. For safety from the wind, I pulled for shore and hauled the canoe up on a dock, where I discovered an old fisherman's shanty. It was early morning still, and I watched the fishermen prepare to go out and collect their nets. Fishing on the Hudson is a vanishing profession: the release of certain pollutants in the last forty years has destroyed the 300-year-old commercial fishing tradition. In fact, the lower river is so polluted that fishermen will catch and sell only certain fish.

The river forms a kind of bay near the Tappan Zee Bridge.

40

Hudson River fishermen heading out at dawn.

JUNE 30 – LEGENDS OF THE VALLEY

The Hudson is an unpredictable river. To the early Dutch sailors the river and the land on either side of it had a mysterious quality. The skippers who sailed up to Albany and back to Manhattan made up tales about the lower Hudson Valley, about the tides and the mountains. One of America's first writers lived here. Washington Irving captured the superstitions of the settlers in his stories. In "Rip Van Winkle," for instance, the valley's many thunder storms were explained as the ghosts of Henry Hudson's crew bowling in the mountains.

The volcanic cliffs that form the Palisades.

JULY 1 – NEW YORK CITY

Just before I reached Englewood boat basin, where I would camp my last night on the river, I canoed beneath the Palisades. The huge volcanic cliffs line the western shore. I followed the river below the cliffs and wondered what would happen to my canoe if a piece of that towering rock fell off. I was only a few miles from the George Washington Bridge that joins New Jersey with Manhattan, but I could not hear the sound of the city yet. Everything was quiet on the river. I was not hindered by traffic. I could stop or continue, rest or paddle. Perhaps this was one of the best things about my trip so far: the freedom out there on the Hudson.

I pitched my tent on a strip of grass in the Englewood marina. I heated up some tea and gazed out across the river at the Spuyten Duyvil Bridge that connects the Bronx to the northern tip of Manhattan.

Approaching the George Washington Bridge.

JULY 2 - MOUTH OF A GREAT RIVER

Up early, I canoed on the ebb tide under the George Washington Bridge. The current grew stronger than ever as I passed over to the Manhattan side of the river. I came upon the remnants of the old piers and run-down docks that were used for commerce years ago when the river was important in the daily lives of New Yorkers. From here the great ships Lusitania and Mauritania sailed. Survivors of the Titanic disaster found refuge on these very piers. This is where immigrants landed before going on to Ellis Island. It is silent now, but many thousands of soldiers said goodbye from these now-broken wharves before sailing overseas.

The tide was so strong I didn't even have to paddle; I just steered. A Circle Line tour boat passed me, and I waved. The tall buildings spiked the sky. Sitting in my canoe at the bottom of the twin towers of the World Trade Center was like sitting at the base of two great, slick mountain walls of glass and steel. I knew I'd come a long way. I'd journeyed from the simple wilderness of evergreens to one of the greatest urban centers in the world.

I passed old piers and run-down docks.

The sea swelled in broad waves, and I braced myself with my paddle, hoping I wouldn't turn over in front of my family, who had come out to greet me. I had canoed for three weeks and covered more than 300 miles. I'd traveled from a lake high in the Adirondack Mountains through whitewater and around dams and into locks, following this wide, historic, diversified river. I'd seen the river as it is today, and I'd gotten a better sense of the way it was yesterday.

Though sea gulls swirled above me by the hundreds, tourists at Battery Park gazing out toward the Atlantic Ocean hardly knew I'd arrived. Far below them, the tide was ripping at the rock of the great city. I too looked at the harbor, and I pictured Henry Hudson returning from his three-week trip upriver nearly 400 years ago. It was here that he set the sails of the Half Moon and headed back to England.

I paddled hard so I wouldn't be swept out to sea. Somehow I maneuvered my canoe to the dock. I jumped out. The canoe bashed into the pilings, but I quickly drew it up onto the cement. Although my journey was over, I would never forget the long trail to Lake Tear of the Clouds, or the wind and roar of whitewater, or the tiring heat of solo paddling, or the fierce tides and wild sea gulls at the end of this great River of the Mountains.

At last I was home.

At the mouth of the river, the mountains are made of glass and steel.

Special thanks to Ernie LaPrairie, Lynn O'Malley, Patty McCool, and Scott Overdorf.

For their photographic contributions, thanks to Jim Swedberg, Pat Shafer, and Jan Cheripko.

Also many thanks to Betsy Folwell, Milda Burns, Helen Donohue, Peter Barton, Herb Helms, Forrest Hartley, Lee Butler, Pete Bishop and his whole family, Joan Patton, Alexis Nadeau, Fred Godfrey, John Cronin and the Riverkeeper staff, Robert Boyle, Robert Stout, and all the others who helped me along the way.

Photographs: Peter Lourie: Pages 1, 2, 4, 7, 8, 10 Left, 17, 19, 20, 21, 22, 24, 25, 26, 27, 30, 3 1, 40, 41, 42, 43; Jim Swedberg: Pages 5, 9, 11, 12, 13, 14, 15, 16, 18; Pat Shafer: Pages 3, 32, 33, 34, 35, 38, 44, 45 , 47; Jan Cheripko: Pages 28, 36, 39, 43; Photograph Page 10 Right courtesy of The Adirondack Museum, Blue Mountain Lake, N.Y. ; Photograph Page 23 courtesy of Finch, Pruyn & Co., Inc., Glens Falls, N.Y.; Photograph Page 29 Courtesy of The New York Historical Society.

Text copyright © 2015 by Peter Lourie
Photographs copyright © 2015 by Peter Lourie except where indicated in credits.
All rights reserved
Published by Snake Mountain Press
Snake Mountain Road
Weybridge, Vermont 05753

Publisher Cataloging-in-Publication Data
Lourie, Peter.
Hudson River : an adventure from the mountains to the sea / by Peter Lourie.
[48] p. : col. ill. ;   cm.
Summary: An account of th e author's 150-mile canoe trip down the Hudson River. Accompanied by color photographs and maps.
ISBN: 978-0-9848637-2-3
1. Hudson River (N.Y. and N.J.)—Juvenile literature. 2. New York (State)—Description and travel—1981—Juvenile literature.
[l. Hudson River (N.Y. and N.J.). 2. New York (State)—Description and travel- 1981-.] 1. Title.
917.47'3—dc20   1992
Library of Congress Catalog Card Number: 91-72870

Snake Mountain Edition, 2015

Original book designed by Abby Kagan.

Made in the USA
San Bernardino, CA
18 March 2015